FOR MY PAL SANDY LIEBERSON

"Now add the sugar."   *"Now add the sugar"...*   *"Now add the sugar"...*

PHILIP COLLINS

PHILIP

THE GOLDEN AGE OF TELEVISIONS

COLLINS

Photography by Garry Brod

Design by Kosh

Publisher: W. Quay Hays

Design: Kosh Design Studios

Editorial Director: Peter L. Hoffman

Production Director: Trudihope Schlomowitz

Prepress Manager: Bill Castillo

Production: Gabriela Lopez, Maritta Tapanainen

Production Assistants: David Chadderdon, Gus Dawson, Roy Penn

A FILLIP BOOK

For information:
General Publishing Group, Inc.
2701 Ocean Park Boulevard, Suite 140
Santa Monica, CA 90405

Library of Congress
Cataloging-in-Publication Data
Collins, Philip, 1944-
      The golden age of televisions / by Philip Collins, ; photography
   by Garry Brod ; design by Kosh.
          p.   cm.
      ISBN 1-57544-019-9
      1. Television--United States--History. 2. Television--United
   States--Receivers and reception--History.   I. Title.
   TK6635.U5C65 1997
   384.55'4'0973--dc21   97-36228
                                    CIP

Printed in the USA by
RR Donnelley & Sons Company
10 9 8 7 6 5 4 3 2 1
General Publishing Group
Los Angeles

CONTENTS

"PEOPLE WILL SOON *get tired of staring at a plywood box every night."* — *Darryl Zanuck, 1946.*

Question: *What do the names Jackson, Fillmore, Monroe, Lincoln, Harrison, Tyler, Adams and Garfield have in common?*

Answer: *They are all Zenith Televisions from the 1950 "Presidential" line of Black Magic TV's with the "Super Range" Chassis. These models with 16" 'porthole' circular screens typified the range of choice on offer from US manufacturers whose names dwindled into obscurity after the initial boom of TV purchasing in the fifties and early sixties. Fada, Dumont, Capeheart, Stewart-Warner, Stromberg-Carlson, Motorola, Sentinel, Silvertone, Philco and Scott are familiar names to anyone who remembers Elvis' first hit. RCA and Zenith are the brand name survivors of an onslaught of Japanese competition that saw Sony and others replace American knowhow with Oriental ingenuity. During the fifties, large wooden consoles that dominated the corner space in our dens and parlors with 7", 9", 12" and 16" screens offering a variety of programming in glorious black and white rapidly replaced radio as the #1 source of news and entertainment for America's middle class during the fifties, reaching 95% penetration of all market sectors by 1960.*

"Television is more interesting than people. If it were not, we should have people standing in the corners of our rooms." — ALAN COREN

While the console radio in its myriad forms—lowboy, highboy, chairside etc—was considered furniture or at least a furnishing accessory, the same cannot be said of television sets. Primarily functional apparatus, cabinet design rarely deviated from a conservative, fairly stark housing for an unwieldy cathode ray tube and a mass of technology that produced a volume of parts four times the size of the average radio chassis. Hence

Fergusson, 1986 (Repro) UK

RCA, TKR-12, 1939 USA

RCA, 1947 USA

Sony, 1959 Japan

cabinets held close to the minimum requirement of size to accommodate a space that still sat handily in the average size living room. Early sets were mostly wooden housing, with polished veneers that harmonized with the furniture. Some bakelite table models were produced in the early fifties as well as a console or two (weighing far more than their compact size suggested), but it was the metal cabinets of the portable sets of the fifties that started to offer colorful alternatives to traditional brown wood veneers. "Leatherette" cloth laminates were also applied to both metal and wood cabinets for table models and portables during this period, and eventually plastic compounds superceded wood, in much the same way as radio cabinetry two decades earlier, although the compact five-tube radios offered far more opportunity for flamboyant design. It is just possible that designers were deliberately concentrating the screen area as the focal point of the TV set to the exclusion of any visual distraction elsewhere. Early consoles, featuring a set of doors to hide the screen when the set was not in use would support this theory. Certainly the screen magnifiers that were commonly used on smaller early sets did nothing to enhance a pleasing design. A large glob of solid glass or a glass bubble filled with oil increased the image size by a couple of inches but detracted from any obvious design feature the cabinet may otherwise have offered. Still, when you're five years old and Wyatt Earp was rounding up the bad guys, who cared?

"Television? No good will come of this device. The word is half Greek and half Latin." — C.P. SCOTT

A standardized screen aspect ratio saw the demise of the porthole screen in favor of a rounded rectangular picture area that roughly scaled down from the nation's cinema screen ratio (excluding CinemaScope and Cinerama). Status was measured not only by the model and year of the automobile that sat in the driveway, but by

the size of the TV screen that sat in the living room. Indeed, the appearance of an external antenna on your roof told the neighbors that even if your name wasn't Jones, you were keeping up with them. The cover of **Fortune** magazine for July 1949 satirizes the mushrooming of TV antennae, depicting an array of bizarrely shaped metal X's, H's, circles and horizontal bars becoming the unfortunate focal point of a row of exquisite 19th century homes. The same issue quotes a research economist opining, "Once the coast-to-coast networks are established, there are few advertisers with manufacturing potentials great enough to warrant using the sales impact of television on a national scale."

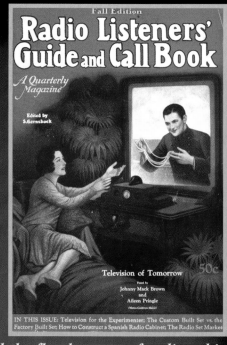

> "I have had my aerials (antennae) removed. It's the moral equivalent of a
> prostate operation." — MALCOLM MUGGERIDGE, 1981

The fifties witnessed enough tubular steel sprouting from the nation's roofs to circle the globe many times. With the introduction of miniaturized electrical circuit boards in 1955, TV design enabled slimmer, more compact table models to induce a hungry public to buy a second set for the kitchen and bedroom. "The box" became more colorful, lighter to handle and altogether more user-friendly; retaining simple, functionary design that while reflecting the influences of the period, never approached the flamboyance of radio cabinetry of the era. Most notable for its design is the landmark range of models offered by Philco in 1958, featuring a swivel screen that conformed to the shape of the cathode ray tube, in a stark plastic housing above the mechanics of the set which were enclosed in various cabinet designs. The "Predicta" range, as it is commonly known, is a high point of TV design, featuring an overall 'futuristic-fifties' concept of space travel and science fiction visions. With unfuturistic names like "Pedestal", "Tandem", "Townhouse" and "Princess", these models are the most collectible and desirable among design and TV enthusiasts. Pre-WWII sets are the most valuable, principally due to their scarcity rather than any design merit. Estimates vary as to the numbers of existing sets from the 1930s—probably as low as 200 in the US and 350 in Great Britain, based upon a survival rate of 2% of known production figures.

> "Television is an invention that permits you to be entertained in your living room by people you wouldn't want
> in your home." — DAVID FROST

Along with the explosion of TV buying in the early fifties came the inevitable ancillary merchandising, not so much as a conscious campaign by TV manufacturers but as a recognition by the rest of the world that this was a phenomenon that outstripped any domestic technology hitherto enjoyed on planet Earth. Hence, an enormous variety of everyday consumer goods carried a TV screen visual identity or were shaped to resemble actual sets. Prominent were toys that housed pencil sharpeners, money banks, miniature viewers, clocks and lamps. Merchandising from programming was produced on an unprecedented scale, from Hopalong Cassidy to The Flintstones and beyond. All of which led Orson Welles to proclaim:"I hate television. I hate it as much as peanuts. But I can't stop eating peanuts."

Baird, Televisor, 1920, UK

General Electric,
Octagon, 1928, USA

1 9 2 5

June 13: Charles Francis Jenkins oversees the first transmission of moving pictures using motion-picture film: the image of a windmill is sent from Anacosta D.C. to Washington D.C., five miles away.

1 9 2 6

August 18: A weather map is televised for the first time, from Arlington, Virginia, radio station NAA, to the Weather Bureau Office in Washington D.C.

1 9 2 7

April 7: TV images are sent over long-distance telephone lines between Washington D.C. and New York City—the first inter-city telecast. Herbert Hoover, Secretary of Commerce, spoke the first words into the telephone. The *New York Times* reported, "It was as if a photograph had suddenly come to life."

1 9 2 8

JANUARY 13: The first American home gets a TV set, in Schenectady, NY. It has a $1^{1}/2$" square screen. **FEBRUARY 8:** John Logie Baird sends the first television image from London, England, to Hartsdale, NY. **MAY 11:** The first regular transmissions, three afternoons a week, commence from the first US TV station, General Electric's WGY. **JUNE:** The first outdoor "location" television shots are taken by John Logie Baird. **AUGUST 13:** WRNY, Coytesville, NJ, becomes the first standard broadcast station to televise an image—the face of Mrs. John Geloso—to an invited audience of 500 assembled in NYU's Philosophy Hall. The image was magnified to 3" square. **AUGUST 21:** The first listing of a TV program appears in the *New York Times.* **AUGUST 22:** The first "remote" television pick up: General Electric engineers televised Governor Alfred E. Smith accepting the Democratic nomination for President in the Capitol Building, Albany, NY.

1 9 2 9

JUNE 27: Bell Telephone Laboratories in NYC demonstrate the first crude color TV pictures: a bouquet of roses and the American flag. **NOVEMBER 18:** Zworykin demonstrates the "Kinescope," an early picture tube whose face is the "screen" of home TV receivers. Images are produced by a stationary electron gun scanning a fluorescent surface.

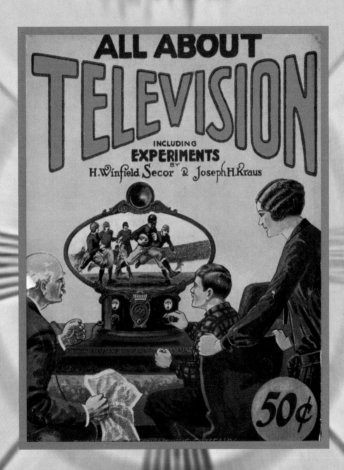

1 9 3 0

MAY 22: An audience at Procter's Theater, Schenectady, becomes the first to see closed-circuit TV projected onto a big screen. **JUNE 30:** W2XBS, NBC's first TV station, transmits live the English Derby. **JULY 21:** W2XAB, CBS' first TV station, starts transmitting in New York, and CBS announces the first regular seven-day-a-week schedule of TV broadcasting in America.

TELEVISION
FUTURE ELECTRICAL EYES

BY RADIO

FROM THE THEATRE
SIGHT AND SOUND TRANSMITTED BY
SENDING APPARATUS

AT THE HOME
IMAGE AND VOICE RECEIVED BY
RECEIVING APPARATUS

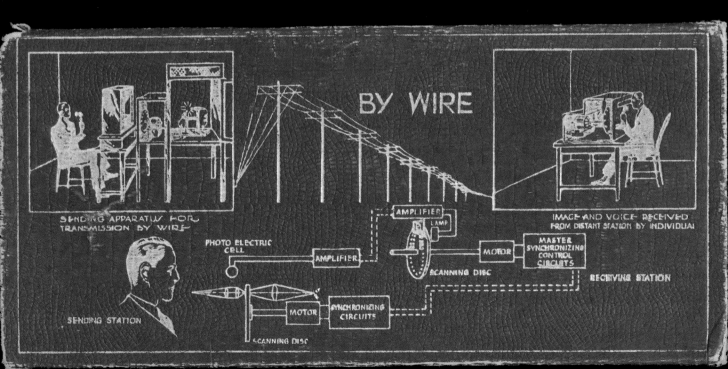

BY WIRE

**SENDING APPARATUS FOR
TRANSMISSION BY WIRE**

**IMAGE AND VOICE RECEIVED
FROM DISTANT STATION BY INDIVIDUAL**

PHOTO ELECTRIC
CELL

AMPLIFIER

AMPLIFIER
LAMP

MOTOR

MASTER
SYNCHRONIZING
CONTROL
CIRCUITS

SCANNING DISC

RECEIVING STATION

SENDING STATION

MOTOR

SYNCHRONIZING
CIRCUITS

SCANNING DISC

Baird, 1936 UK

Cosser, 1936 UK

1 9 3 7 DECEMBER 12: NBC and RCA send the first mobile TV vans onto the streets of New York City.

November 15: NBC's mobile TV van televises the first (and unscheduled) news event live on location: a fire at a barracks in New York.

HMV, 1938 UK

RADIO NEWS

MAY
25 Cents

Over 200
Illustrations

REG. U.S. PAT. OFF.

Edited by HUGO GERNSBACK

$300.00
IN PRIZES
What's Wrong
WITH THIS
PICTURE?
See Page 1328

RADIO'S GREATEST MAGAZINE

EXPERIMENTER PUBLISHING COMPANY, NEW YORK, PUBLISHERS OF
SCIENCE & INVENTION · RADIO LISTENERS' GUIDE · AMAZING STORIES · MONEY MAKING · RADIO INTERNACIONAL

RADIO'S LIVEST MAGAZINE

Special
Broadcast
Number

Radio-Craft

HUGO GERNSBACK, Editor

THE RADIO SET
OF 1950
See Page 458

Novelty Radio Sets — Radio in Model Homes — Versatile Test Unit
How Broadcast Artists Record Their Programs — Contracted Speech

Fall Edition

Radio Listeners' Guide and Call Book

A Quarterly Magazine

Edited by
S. Gernsback

Television of Tomorrow

Posed by
Johnny Mack Brown
and
Aileen Pringle
(Metro-Goldwyn-Mayer)

IN THIS ISSUE: Television for the Experimenter; The Custom Built Set vs. the Factory Built Set; How to Construct a Spanish Radio Cabinet; The Radio Set Market

RADIO'S LIVEST MAGAZINE

Special Television Number

Radio-Craft

August
25 Cents
Canada 30c

HUGO GERNSBACK Editor

MULTIPLE-IMAGE TELEVISION RECEIVER
See Page 74

Television in the U. S., Canada, Europe and Japan—Cathode-Ray Tubes
Making a Facsimile Apparatus—"Frequency" vs. "Amplitude" Modulation

General Electric, 1939 USA

1 9 3 9

RCA televises the opening of the World's Fair in New York. Speeches by President Roosevelt and RCA president David Sarnoff are high-lights. MAY 17: The first baseball game to be televised is a victory for Princeton over Columbia, 2-1, an NBC broadcast called by Bill Stern. June 1: The first televised prize fight—Lou Nova versus Max Baer. The venue is Yankee Stadium. Nova won in 11 rounds. JUNE 20: NBC broadcasts the first musical to be shown on regularly scheduled TV: " The Pirates of Penzance." AUGUST 26: W2XBS televises the first major league baseball game: Brooklyn Dodgers versus the Cincinnati Reds at Ebbets Field. SEPTEMBER 30: W2XBS televises the first college football game: Fordham versus Waynesburg.

THE *Television*

By EDWARD M. NOLL

Part 4. The fundamental operation of various r.f., i.f., and video stages that are employed in present day television receivers.

DuMont, 1945 USA

SUCCESSFUL
DEALER

TELEVISION   RADIO

1 9 4 0

FEBRUARY 1: NBC transmits the first official network-television broadcast, from New York City to station **W2XBS**, a distance of about 130 miles. **FEBRUARY 28: W2XBS** televises first basketball game—a double header, Pittsburgh v. Fordham and NYU v. Georgetown, from Madison Square Garden. **JUNE 24:** The Republican political convention in Philadelphia becomes the first to be televised.

RCA, 1939 & 1946 USA

1 9 4 1

JANUARY: TV sets are selling at the rate of about 90 per month. **MAY 3:** The FCC approves a 525-line definition, 30 pictures per second standard for black & white TV broadcast and reception. **JULY 1:** Commercial TV begins with **CBS' WCBW** and **NBC's WNBT.** The first TV commercial is aired—a 10-second Bulova Watch Time announcement superimposed over a test pattern at a cost of $9.00. **DECEMBER 7: CBS** televises news of the attack on Pearl Harbor.

1 9 4 5

Swiss inventor, Hans Laube, experiments with "Smellovision," in which a "smell pack" was stimulated by television waves to produce an odor appropriate to what was on the screen at the time. MARCH 21: Nine commercial stations are in operation in the US: three in New York City, two each in Chicago and Hollywood, one each in Philadelphia and Schenectady. OCTOBER 24 to NOVEMBER 14: The first public TV demonstration in Gimbels Department store, Philadelphia, attracts more than 25,000 eager viewers.

Admiral, 1947 & 1948 USA

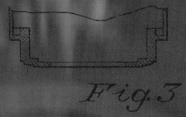

Fig.3

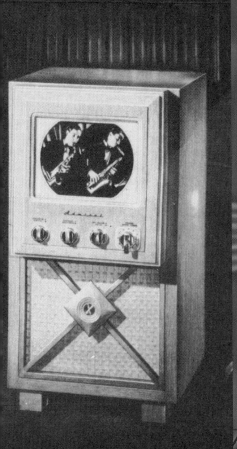

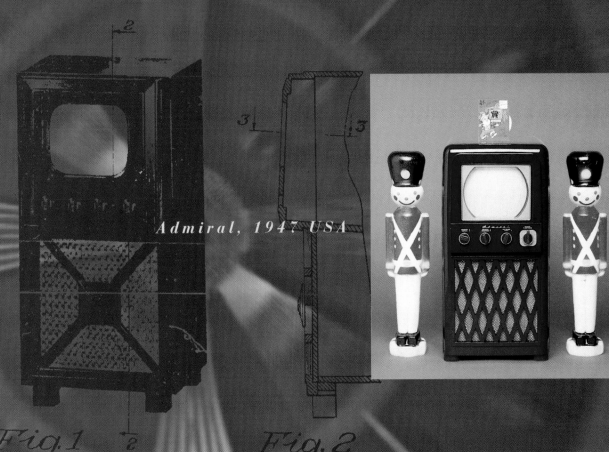

Admiral, 1947 USA

Fig.1

Fig.2

Admiral

INVENTOR.
Samuel E. Adler
BY
J. D. Douglas
Atty.

1946

MAY 9: "Hourglass," the first hour-long musical-variety program airs over NBC's three stations—New York City, Philadelphia and Schenectady. JUNE 19: The first televised heavyweight title fight (Joe Louis v. Billy Conn) is viewed by a record 140,000. One year later, the Louis-Walcott fight is viewed by 1,000,000. OCTOBER 2: "Faraway Hills" becomes the first TV soap opera, airing on the new DuMont network, a broadcaster that also produces the hardware, DuMont television sets.

RCA, 1946 USA

again present our
Progress Map with
ons because many
rested us to supply
form that it may
ntly displayed.
ose of the map is
aler in the United
where located, to
oself and his cus-

No one knows when
ted to these applicants,
fact that it will be
r licenses have been
ny station would be
. out.

POTS These indicate
more of the country's
sting stations are lo-

Motorola, 1947/49 USA

TELEVISION STATIONS
LICENSED and COMPLETED

TELEVISION STATIONS
LICENSED and NEARING COMPLETION

TELEVISION STATIONS
LICENSED

TELEVISION STATION
LICENSES APPLIED FOR

REGULAR RADIO STATIONS

Necessity for Concentrated Audience Within Its Limited   Range

RADIO *and Television* RETAILING, MAY, 1939

TELEVISION PROGRESS M
Where Stations Are Ready, Under Construction, Proposed (

RADIO *and Television* **RETAILING**

Television Initially to Big Cities, While Radio Continues to Cover the Country

Farnsworth, 1947 USA

1 9 4 7

Approximately 44,000 TV sets in the US, and over 40,000,000 radios. MAY 7: Kraft Television Theater begins its distinguished run on NBC, becoming the first commercial TV dramatic series. SEPTEMBER 13: The idea of syndicating TV series takes form as Eastman Kodak and NBC develop a film camera for shooting off the TV screen, permitting the recording and later distribution of live shows for sale, or archiving. The films are called "kinescopes." September 30: The first telecast of a World Series game between the New York Yankees and the Brooklyn Dodgers (the Subway series) was seen in New York City, Washington D.C., Philadelphia and Schenectady by approximately 4,000,000 (3.5 million of them in restaurants and bars). October 5: Harry Truman becomes the first president to make a presidential address to the public on TV from the White House. He discusses the international food crisis, proposing meatless Tuesdays. NOVEMBER 6: "Meet the Press" premieres as a local offering on NBC's Washington station. On NOVEMBER 20, it went Network. DECEMBER 29: Say kids! What time is it? Howdy Doody Time! For the first time on NBC.

PLAYTIME TEL-O-VISION
INSTRUCTIONS

GENERAL:

Every effort has been made in the design and ma[nufacture of] Tel-O-Vision to make it a safe, durable, and la[sting educa-]tional play value.

SAFETY:

This toy has been laboratory ins[pected by] Laboratories, Inc. and the Canadian S[...]

For your protection each unit [...] to insure against any possible wir[ing...]

OPERATING INSTRUCTIONS

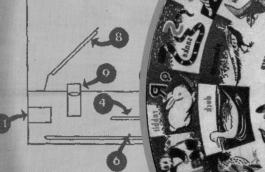

Play-Time TEL-O-VISION

Alphabet and Numbers

Row 1 - Animals
Row 2 - Birds
Row 3 - Fish

Manufactured by HANDY MFG. CO., WORCESTER, MASS.

1. KNOB 4. SHA[FT]
2. BEAD 5. RUB[BER]
3. FOCUS CAM 6. PIN

1. Raise shaft (4) to allow acc[ess]
2. Insert Disc with pictures facin[g]
3. Plug cord into an electric outlet,

CONTROLS:

1. To select picture row on disc, move [...]
2. Turn knob (1) to rotate disc and selec[t]
3. Rotate focus cam (3) to left or right to ob[...]
   The purpose of this control is to compensate [...] discs which may become bent in use.

PARTS SERVICE:

Replacement parts may be obtained at a nominal cost from the Handy Manu-facturing Co., Inc., 80 Webster St., Worcester, Mass. or the Peter-Austin Mfg. Ltd., 314-316 Davenport Rd., Toronto, Canada. Order parts by name and number from [...] diagram.

Philco, 1947 USA

General Electric, 1948/1949 USA

Viewtone, 1947 USA

Baird, 1948 UK Capehart, 1949 USA

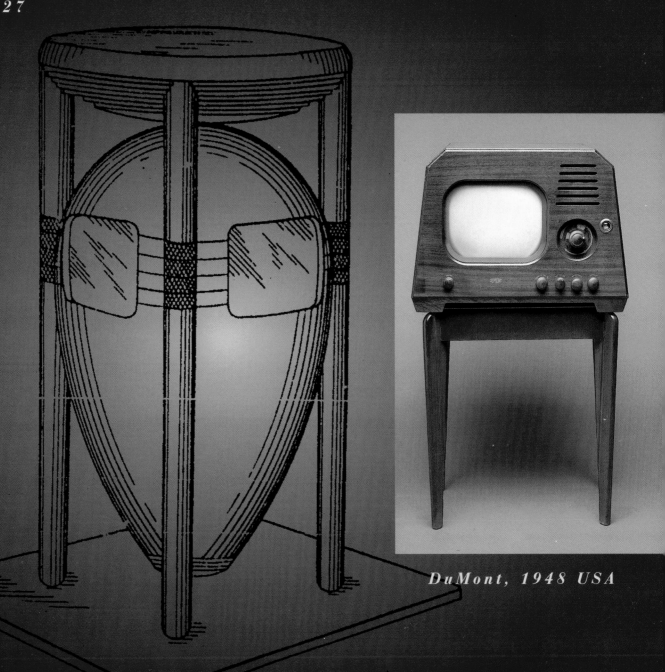

Television receiver,
patent design #157,327
November, 1948 USA

DuMont, 1948 USA

General Electric, 1948 USA

Motorola, 1948 USA

G.E.C., 1950 USA

Philco, 1948 USA

1 9 4 8

An estimated 600,000 TV sets in America are now tuned in to 45 stations, nationwide. FEBRUARY: ABC forms a four-station network. AUGUST 10: "Candid Camera" debuts on ABC. Later, a regular on CBS. AUGUST 15: CBS inaugurates the first nightly news broadcast for a network, "CBS-TV News" with Douglas Edwards, but is unable to attract any sponsors. AUGUST 27: Alger Hiss is accused of being a Communist while appearing on "Meet the Press." A landmark court case ensues. SEPTEMBER: It is estimated that one third of the US population is within reach of a TV station. SEPTEMBER 21: "Uncle Miltie" takes America by storm. Milton Berle headlines the first Texaco Star Theatre, and soon captures 92% of the viewing audience. Two years later, with more competition, his audience share is at 81%. NOVEMBER 29: "Kukla, Fran and Ollie" premieres on NBC.

PHILCO TELEVISION

HORIZONTAL BAR CONTROL
VERTICAL CENTER KNOB   OFF-ON   CONTRAST   BRIGHTNESS   CHANNEL SELECTOR
VOLUME

Hofman, 1949 USA

...ES CLEAR AS THE MOVIES...

FIRST WITH THE FINEST IN TELEVISION

1949

The DuMont Club 20-inch TV set "With the world's largest direct-view screen: 213 sq. inches" goes on sale for $999. FEBRUARY: Bills are introduced in the NY state legislature to permit tenants in apartment buildings to place antennas on their roofs. In other states, laws are passed prohibiting the installation of TV sets in automobiles. APRIL 30: ABC announces "the television development of the year." It has signed "The Lone Ranger" for 52 weekly ½ hours at an inclusive cost of $750,000, creating a record fee for single ½ hour shows. JUNE 27: Get out your decoder rings! "Captain Video" debuts on the DuMont Network.

AUGUST: More than 2,000,000 sets in the US are now in operation; 720,000 in New York City alone. AUGUST 25: RCA announces the development of its color-TV system that is compatible with b/w sets and would not require owners to purchase adapters so their monochrome sets could receive shows televised in color. OCTOBER 10: "Kukla, Fran and Ollie" is broadcast in color via NBC—the first regularly scheduled network show to be received by both color and black-and-white sets. DECEMBER: The #1 household gift is a TV set. The most popular size is a 12½" screen. Sales are 600% ahead of 1948. DECEMBER: Sales of "Howdy Doody" merchandising top $11 million for the year.

Firestone, 1950 USA

Truetone, 1950 USA

Airline, 1949 USA

Sentinels, 1948 USA

Radiola, 1949 USA

Bush, 1950 UK

Bush, 1954 UK

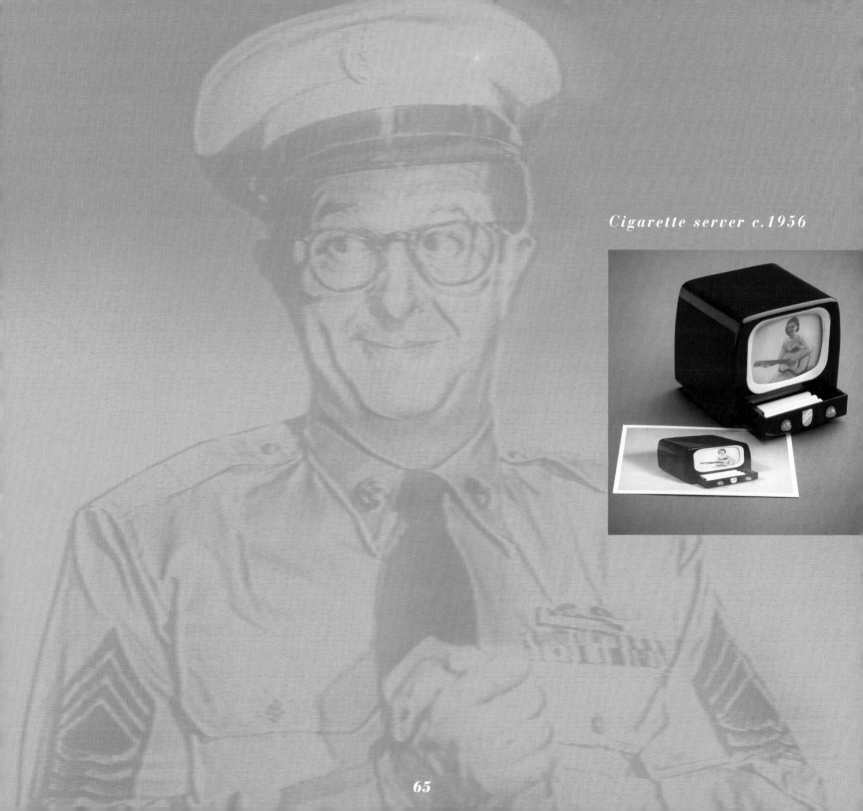

Cigarette server c.1956

La Voix de Son Maitre, 1949 France

Raytheon, 1948 USA

FEBRUARY 25: "Your Show of Shows," starring Sid Caesar, Imogene Coca, Carl Reiner and Howard Morris, premieres on NBC. Arguably the funniest TV series ever. **APRIL:** According to NBC, 5,343,000 TV sets are now in American homes. 500,000 were sold in March alone. 103 TV stations now service 60 markets. **MAY:** The city of Cleveland reports a deficit of $140,677 on its trolley system, citing TV viewing as the cause. Everyone is staying home in front of the TV. **SEPTEMBER 1:** There are now 7,535,000 TV sets in the US. **SEPTEMBER 1:** XEW-TV, Mexico City, acquires the rights to "La Hora de Jeudi Dudi" (Howdy Doody in Spanish) **OCTOBER 1:** Approximately 8,000,000 TVs in the US are now served by 107 stations. **OCTOBER 7:** Frank Sinatra flops in his debut show, competing against "Your Show of Shows" and later, Milton Berle on the Texaco Star Theatre. **OCTOBER 12:** "The George Burns and Gracie Allen Show" debuts on CBS as a fortnightly series. Jack Benny commences a brilliant TV career on CBS with "The Jack Benny Show."

Baird, 1950 UK

Money bank/viewer c.1950

1951

JANUARY 1: Zenith begins a 90-day test of Phonevision in Chicago. 300 selected TV families will be able to see relatively new feature films by dialing a special number on phone circuits attached to their TV sets. The sets will then be able to receive an exclusive channel showing the movie for $1. Viewers without attachments will get a scrambled signal. Major film companies, however, refuse permission for Zenith to continue playing first-run films, fearful that Phonevision will destroy movie theatres. FEBRUARY: The DuMont network establishes the first international TV hookup, linking with Union Radio Television in Havana broadcasting sports programming. MAY 3: NBC gives Milton Berle an unprecedented 30 year, $100,000 per year contract to perform a minimum of 360 shows. He fulfills this requirement by June, 1956. JUNE 28: "Amos 'n' Andy" premieres on CBS. JUNE 14: 13,000,000 sets are now operating in the US. JULY 21: The NAACP protests the TV version of "Amos 'n' Andy," calling it a "gross libel on the Negro and a distortion of the truth." SEPTEMBER 4: The first coast-to-coast transmission (film was employed for one coast prior to this) featured President Truman addressing the Peace Treaty Conference in San Francisco. 107 steel and concrete towers spaced 28 miles apart between New York and San Francisco pass the TV signal via microwave relays. An estimated 14,670,000 viewers watch. OCTOBER 15: "Lucy! I'm home!..." "I Love Lucy" premieres on CBS.

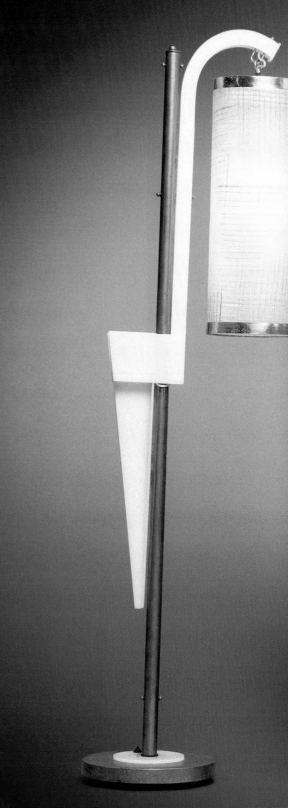

Stromberg Carlson, 1950 USA

Raytheon, 1950 USA

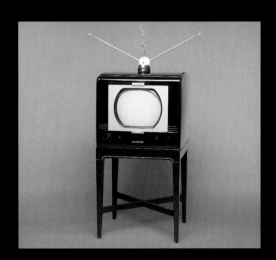

RCA, 1950 USA

Emersons, 1950 USA

ospective Tele

e Sensational N

h, the first of a series of pe

ew York Times. This is the opening gun of Tele King's contemplated

ampaign that will reach prospective television buyers, coast to coast.

20" Model 201: Black rectangular no-glare tube, mahogany veneer cabinet.

Motorola, 1950 USA

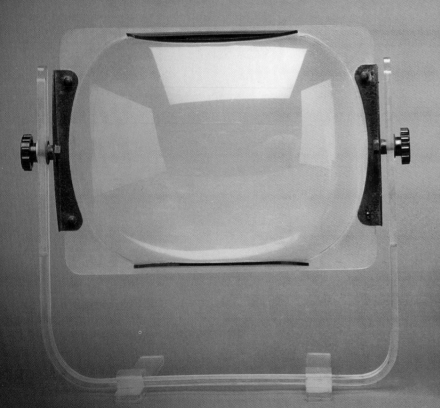

"Sells for me...
BIG!"

Pye, 1950 UK

TELEVIEWING IS A SCIENCE

Up in **Connecticut,** *a dog has, reputedly, gone cross-eyed from watching television. There has been talk of two new spinal ailments—"telesquat" and "telecrane." Stores in major cities are referring guardedly to eye troubles brought on by watching TV, and are marketing tinted and colored "television glasses" to combat the diseases. It has been widely said that glaucoma and other dread eye afflictions are caused by the pernicious TV screen. Worst of all is the persistent rumor (started, says one wag, by a Hollywood agent) that radiations similar to x-rays come out of the face of a TV tube and will, in time, cause sterility, cancer or both.*

But if you've just bought, or want to buy, a TV set, you can rest easy. A lot of good scientific minds have been looking into the matter these days, and their findings are thoroughly reassuring.

That dog story, for instance, is probably just a case of coincidence. Dr. Franklin Foote of the National Society for the Prevention of Blindness says watching TV is no more dangerous than reading—and recent tests show that a normal person can regularly read for six hours at a time without damage. In fact, those who feel eyestrain after an hour of televiewing under optimum conditions probably should have their eyes checked, since it is possible that this hour is the only concentrated use they give their eyes all day. Dr. Foote adds that when you're bored, you often feel as though you have eye fatigue. What the dog was watching is not on record, but it easily could have been one of those moth-eaten vaudeville shows.

All those scare rumors, in fact, are total phonies—just part of the growing pains of America's amazing new industry. As far as you're concerned, you can safely ignore the old wives' tales and look at TV to your heart's content—if you do a little intelligent planning and follow a few simple rules.

First thing is to select a set to fit your room. Screen size, like the length of an automobile hood, seems to be an index of social standing these days; but if you have a small room, you'd be foolish to get too large a screen. Eye specialists agree on one thing: you shouldn't sit too close to the image. The trouble is that the eyes tire to keep in focus an entire area all at once. You can be near a small area, or far from a big one, without damage. According to Dr. Walter King of Buffalo, if you multiply the screen diameter by ten and sit at least that far from the screen, you'll be sitting in the right place. If, in other words, you have a ten-inch screen, sit about eight feet away. Obviously, therefore, if your room won't allow for sitting far back in comfort, a big screen is wrong for you.

Second thing in choosing a set is the color of the set itself, and of the walls. Here again all eye specialists agree: the less contrast between screen brilliance and background, the better for your eyes. The eye continually wrestles to adjust to that contrast; the less there is, the less eye work. That means you should plan on light-colored walls behind the set, and pick a light wood cabinet if you can. Most important of all, arrange your lamps so as to ensure a good, diffused light throughout the room. All those jokes about watching TV in the dark and wondering who's been to your house for the evening are passé. People who know just don't turn out the lights when they teleview.

So, with the proper distance from the screen, you've eliminated fear of eyestrain; and with proper room illumination and light backgrounds, you've gotten rid of any need for "television glasses" or tinted filters, which only serve to dim a bright image. But you still may suffer from "telesquat" and "telecrane" if you try to tuck your TV set right into a room already planned for the old way of life.

Let's admit it: TV, all by itself, is going to revolutionize the evening habits of the American people. In the bridge era, people wanted open floor space for the card tables and chairs. Or the gin-and-tonic type, given to bearskin rugs and languid redheads, planned their rooms about the fireplace. But TV is demanding, and almost hypnotic— you've got to watch it when it's on. Your room has to be built around that tube, if you and your friends aren't to get a bent spine (telesquat) and a pain in the neck (telecrane). And that's not mentioning wear and tear on furniture and rugs, if stuff has to be shoved around for each viewing.

With traditional furniture, the best trick yet is to place the set in a corner. That way, viewers along the two opposite walls can see the set and still talk to each other. When the set goes off, the room doesn't look like a movie house, and no changes need be made.

If you have room enough, though, you can place the set in the middle of one wall—like the traditional fireplace— with a club chair on either side of it and the sofa opposite. (You have to move the chairs to a better distance, however, for viewing.) If you happen to have both a fireplace and a TV set, suggests waggish artist Nino Repetto, you can have a two-faced couch in the middle of the floor, and let some guests roast chestnuts in the fire while others, back-to-back with them, get their chestnuts from Milton Berle.

Whatever you do, though, be sure that the set's high enough to be seen easily, without slumping on the small of the back. Smart designers of several dozen different lines of furniture have made up low-slung "television chairs" that handle the problem nicely. Some even have cocktail arms, which have plenty of room for a glass and an ash tray. If you're stuck with traditional, higher sitting chairs and sofa, get a higher TV table or put a base under your floor model.

Your best bet is to refurnish your room with pieces designed just for the purpose. New sectional sofas are basic for the long, narrow room. To teleview, you shift the sections apart, slant them around facing the set, and thus achieve a theatre-type of seating with little trouble. Odd chairs in the modern lightweight style, with curved plywood back and seat, are good too. They can be moved around with one hand and don't take up much room.

Designer William Pahlmann is one teleminded gent who has put low chairs, sectional sofas, and coffee tables on five-inch rubber castering wheels. A room arranged for conversation can be whisked around into a theatre with no effort at all, and no wear on the rug.

Don't get too comfortable, though. Even though top opthalmologists like Dr. Benjamin Rones of Washington say you won't get eye diseases from TV, they do say you can tire your eyes by too long, uninterrupted watching. Some advise looking away from the set occasionally: others think that's just a psychological trick. A recent survey by a New Jersey research group found that many televiewers claim they feel eyestrain—but nearly half admitted they felt it only after more than three hours of continuous viewing.

But, in line with what Dr. Foote has said about boredom making you seem to feel eyestrain, maybe the best advice is to choose your program instead of prescription. If you're too lazy to flip the channel switch, you deserve whatever headaches you get.

Esquire magazine, 1950

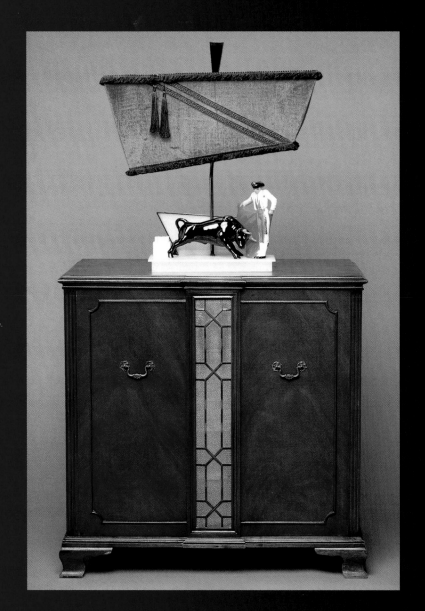

Zenith, 1951 USA

1 9 5 2

JANUARY: Dave Garroway hosts NBC's pioneering "Today Show." APRIL 7: The first TV show to achieve penetration in over 10,000,000 homes is this evening's episode of "I Love Lucy." ABC Research Bureau pegs the number at 10.6 million. APRIL 14: The FCC sets up UHF (ultra high frequency) channels 14 through 83 and certain stations for educational programming. NOVEMBER: RCA demonstrates an experimental TV set using transistors instead of tubes.

1 9 5 3

MAY 24: Paddy Chayefsky's "Marty" starring Rod Steiger airs as an episode of "Goodyear TV Playhouse." A landmark achievement. SEPTEMBER 1: 25,233,000 TV sets now sit in American homes, an estimated 50% of all US households. NOVEMBER 22: "The Colgate Comedy Hour" is the first program to be telecast in color—the RCA compatible color system.

WITH

Admi...

MAGIC MIRROR TE...

RADIOS · TELEVISION · RECORD PLAYE...

Maryland RADIO $370

". . . and this one has everything"

Pictures clear as the movies

Single control station selector

Complete 12-channel coverage

...Chassis

...ARDS OF PERFORMANCE

...es clear as the movies...that's what you get ...ral Magic Mirror Television. Revolutionary ...s assures outstanding performance even in ...eas where ordinary sets fail. Switching from ...station is as easy as tuning a radio. Unique ...gain control" reduces station selection to a ...rol. Also eliminates "flutter" and "breathing" ...used by airplanes overhead. Turret tuner, ...another Admiral development, can readily be adapted to new channels. Direct-view, full-vision picture screens range in size from 7", 10", 12½", up to 16". Choose your Admiral Magic Mirror Television now! The longer you wait, the more fun you miss!

1 9 5 4

MARCH: There are now 370 TV stations on the air with another 202 licensed for future transmission. MARCH: Pall Mall cigarettes produce the first color commercial shown on a color show, sponsored by them. DECEMBER: The last year for the DuMont network, who cannot compete with the rich cash infusion enjoyed by the big three.

RCA, 1954 USA

1 9 5 5

JUNE 7: CBS debuts "The $64,000 Question" hosted by Hal March. It becomes the most watched cult hit of early TV. SEPTEMBER 10: "Gunsmoke" on CBS begins it's 20-year run. John Wayne introduces James Arness in a special insert. SEPTEMBER 20: CBS now unleashes Sgt. Bilko in "The Phil Silvers Show" ("You'll Never Get Rich"). SEPTEMBER 20: ABC premiere of "Cheyenne" starring Clint Walker. OCTOBER 1: CBS debuts a new ½ hour film version of "The Honeymooners," previously a segment in Jackie Gleason's variety show. OCTOBER 3: "The Mickey Mouse Club" is first seen on ABC. OCTOBER 3: CBS debuts "Captain Kangaroo."

Cover drawing by P. Barlow; © 1955
The New Yorker Magazine, Inc.

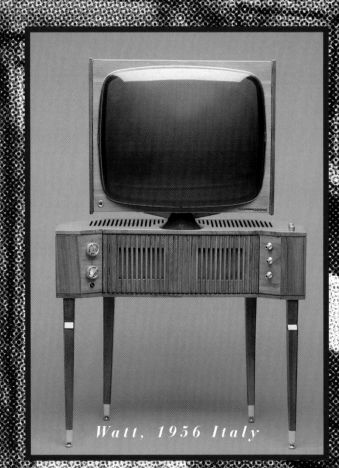

Watt, 1956 Italy

1 9 5 6

APRIL 2: "As The World Turns" starts rolling as CBS' #1 daytime serial. AUGUST 13: CBS, NBC and ABC cover the Chicago Democratic Convention, utilizing tiny TV cameras (5" and 1½ lbs.) and wristwatch microphones. October 11: Rod Serling's "Requiem for a Heavyweight" is presented on CBS' "Playhouse 90," a classic "Golden Age" drama. NOVEMBER: CBS first utilizes videotape in a broadcast, presaging the death of the kinescope.

WEGA, 1956 Germany

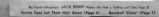

Zenith, 1956 USA

The Saturday Evening

POST

November 9, 1957 - 15¢

HOW TO WIN AT POKER
By Herbert O. Yardley

Michigan's Soapy Williams

JOHN FALTER

THE COVER

Young Sammy Sixgun, using the classic hat-over-the-rock routine, will now restore law and order to the old TV-West. First the electronic badman will shoot a hole through Sammy's sombrero; then, believing he has dispatched its occupant, he will relax his guard and our hero will give him the works. To be sure, this is all good clean imagination. Manhood will find our once-warlike Sammy perched peacefully behind a desk, no heroics for him, no interest in gunplay— yet bearing in him that old spirit which has always turned war-hating Americans into heroes when badmen threaten and the chips are down. By the way, that's John Falter's own dog in the chair, name of Ralph. If Ralph should wag his tail and knock off the hat, wouldn't Sammy be surprised?

RCA, 1957 USA

1 9 5 7

June: 41,000,000 homes have TV sets and 39,000,000 homes receive daily newspapers. TV becomes a major source of news for the American public. **September 21:** "Perry Mason" first appears on CBS. **October 4:** "Leave it to Beaver" premieres on CBS.

RECEIVING BAND V SIGNALS

Practical
Television

1/3

AND TELEVISION TIMES

JULY: 1958

EDITOR: F.J. CAMM

Contents

HEATER-CATHODE TUBE SHORTS

ITV IN DIFFICULT AREAS

UNIVERSAL ALIGNMENT METHOD

A 600 Mc/s OSCILLATOR

A CUBICAL AERIAL FOR TV

Modern Television Receiver Design

Modern Television Receiver Design

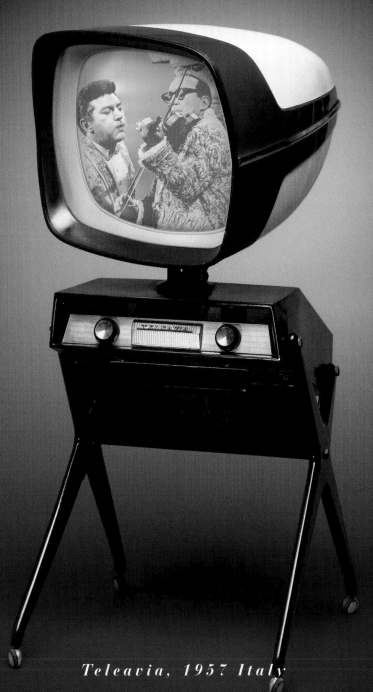

Teleavia, 1957 Italy

RCA, 1957 USA

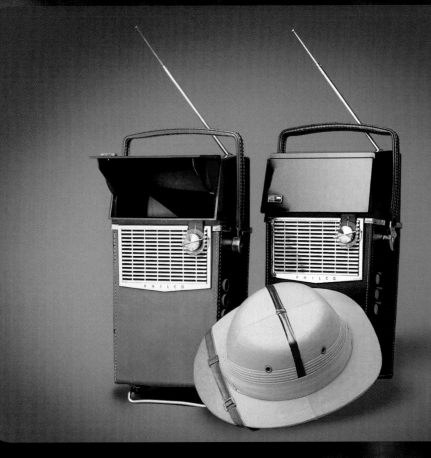

Philco, 1959 USA

1 9 5 8

JANUARY: **TV** is blamed for the decline in movie admissions, down from a peak of 90,000,000 to 30,000,000. JUNE: Trigger retires (age 25). A new "Trigger" steps in. SEPTEMBER 22: "Peter Gunn" is first aired on **NBC**. OCTOBER 17: "An Evening with Fred Astaire" airs on **NBC**. It later wins nine Emmys for the 59-year-old dancer.

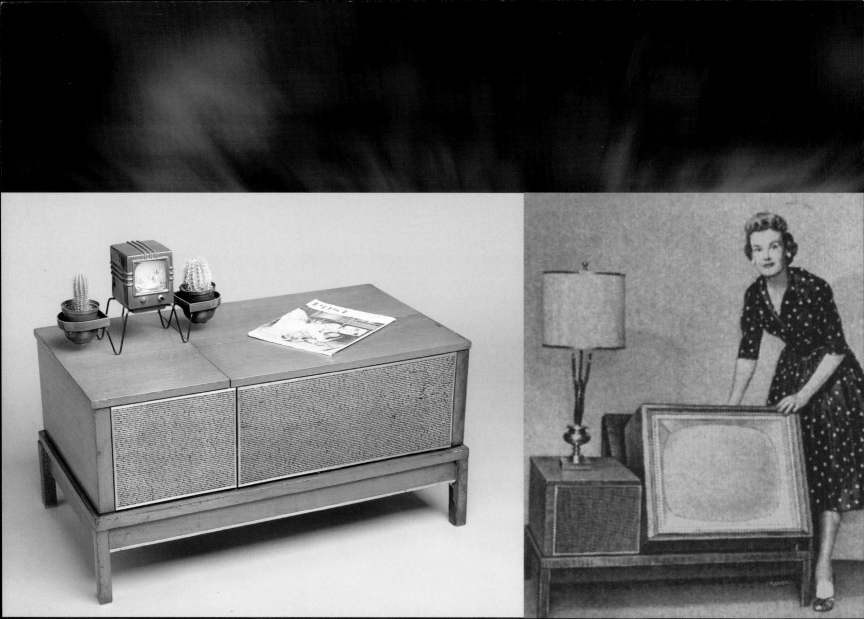

SONY

Sony, 1959 Japan

1 9 5 9

JANUARY 9: "Rawhide" starts its seven-year cattle drive on CBS. FEBRUARY: 50,000,000 TV sets are now in 42,000,000 homes. SEPTEMBER 12: "Bonanza" is the first Western to be broadcast in color for NBC. SEPTEMBER 29: CBS debuts "The Many Loves of Dobie Gillis." OCTOBER 2: "The Twilight Zone" flickers onto the screen for the first time, on CBS. DECEMBER: For the first time, annual TV commercial time sales ($1,240,000,000) exceed motion picture box office receipts ($1,235,000,000) for the year.

FEBRUARY: CBS adopts a mandatory policy for all its stations to present frequent editorials to "serve the public interest by stimulating thinking and decision making about important public issues." **SEPTEMBER 24:** Goodbye, "Howdy Doody," after 13 years and 2,343 shows. **SEPTEMBER 26:** Kennedy and Nixon square off in the first of several televised "Great Debates." **SEPTEMBER 30:** "The Flintstones," the first primetime cartoon series, debuts on ABC. **OCTOBER 7:** "Route 66" premieres on CBS

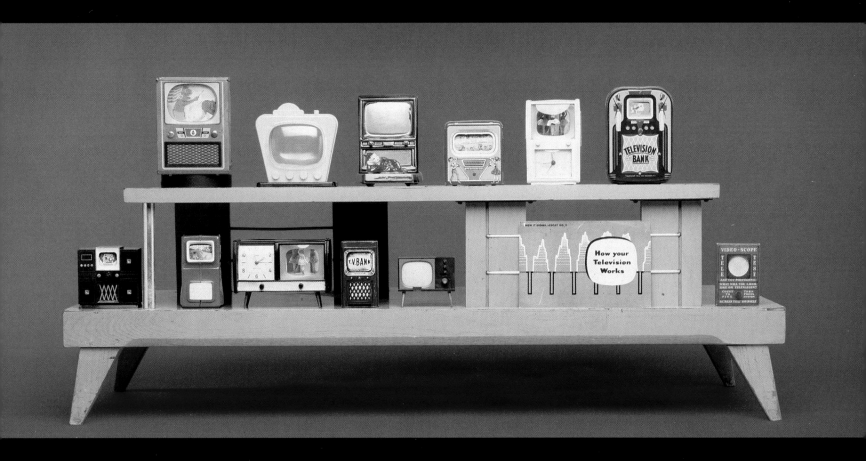

1961

APRIL: There are 600,000 color TV sets in America's 47,000,000 homes, and only one network, NBC, broadcasting in color. The network is owned by RCA, who dominates the production of color TV sets. **APRIL 29:** ABC's "Wide World of Sports" makes its debut. "The thrill of victory...the agony of defeat." **MAY 9:** FCC Chairman, Newton Minow, calls TV a "vast wasteland" at the Broadcaster's Convention. **SEPTEMBER 28:** "Dr. Kildare" premieres on NBC. **OCTOBER 3:** CBS presents the first "Dick Van Dyke Show."

1962

FEBRUARY 14: Jacqueline Kennedy takes the American public on a tour of the White House on both CBS and NBC. ABC screens it two nights later. APRIL 16: Walter Cronkite becomes CBS' news anchorman. SEPTEMBER 23: "The Jetsons" fly out on ABC. SEPTEMBER 26: "The Beverly Hillbillies" drive into the neighborhood on CBS. OCTOBER 1: Johnny Carson takes over as host of "The Tonight Show." OCTOBER: Lucille Ball settles into a regular Monday night slot on CBS.

1963

FEBRUARY 22: Pebbles Flintstone is born to Fred and Wilma. 250,000 Pebbles dolls are manufactured to celebrate. SEPTEMBER 17: Dr. Richard Kimble starts his quest for the one-armed man in "The Fugitive" on ABC—a four-year search. SEPTEMBER 17: "My Favorite Martian" is born on CBS. NOVEMBER 22–25: The assassination of President Kennedy becomes television's momentous news reportage occasion of the century

1964

FEBRUARY 9: The Beatles play "The Ed Sullivan Show." MARCH 20: "Jeopardy!" premieres on NBC. APRIL 30: All TV sets manufactured for domestic use must now receive UHF (Ultra High Frequency—channels 14–83 in addition to the VHF channels.) SEPTEMBER 15: "Peyton Place" arrives on ABC. SEPTEMBER 17: "Bewitched" starts its magic on ABC. SEPTEMBER 18: "The Addams Family" is introduced on ABC. SEPTEMBER 22: "The Man From U.N.C.L.E." debuts on NBC. SEPTEMBER 24: "The Munsters" start to spoof on NBC. SEPTEMBER 26: "Gilligan's Island" commences its run on CBS.

1965

JANUARY 1: On WNEW-TV in New York, Soupy Sales exhorts his kiddie viewers to go into their daddies' wallets and remove "those little green pieces of paper with pictures of George Washington, Benjamin Franklin, Lincoln and Jefferson on them, send them to me, and I'll send you a postcard from Puerto Rico." After a deluge of paper money, Sales is suspended by the station, but is reinstated after another deluge of viewer outrage. JANUARY 12: "Hullabaloo" makes its rock & roll debut on NBC. AUGUST: There are now 51,000,000 TV sets in the US, 3,600,000 of which receive color. SEPTEMBER 15: "Green Acres" premieres on CBS. SEPTEMBER 15: Bill Cosby becomes the first black actor to appear on a regular drama series, "I Spy," on CBS. SEPTEMBER 17: "Hogan's Heroes" starts its run on CBS. SEPTEMBER 18: "Get Smart," would you believe? premieres on NBC. NOVEMBER 8: "Days of Our Lives" replaces "Moment of Truth" on NBC.

1966

JANUARY 12: ABC premieres "Batman." *Pow!* FEBRUARY: An estimated 189,837,950 TV sets worldwide. Most are in the US, followed by Japan and Russia. MAY 8: "Death of a Salesman" is recreated on CBS starring Lee J. Cobb and Mildred Dunnock. SEPTEMBER 8: "Star Trek" starts to beam up on NBC.

Philco, 1962 USA

1 9 6 7

JANUARY 12: "Dragnet" returns to NBC with new episodes after a seven-year hiatus. JUNE 25: National Education TV participates in a two-hour live show "Our World" from 19 nations on five continents, seen simultaneously in 30 countries via four satellites. It is the first global television hookup in history, featuring Japanese shrimp farming, Rachmaninov, and the Beatles among the many sequences. AUGUST 29: Dr. Richard Kimble finds his man on "The Fugitive" and 72% of all TVs are tuned in. SEPTEMBER 9: "Rowan & Martin's Laugh In" explodes on NBC. NOVEMBER 5: PBS commences its quality programming via a network of 119 education stations with the "Public Broadcast Laboratory," hosted by Edward P. Morgan.

1 9 6 8

JUNE 1: "The Prisoner" debuts on CBS. SEPTEMBER 15: The new season is the first to air feature films in prime time every night of the week. SEPTEMBER 17: "Julia," the first comedy series to star a black actress, Diahann Carroll, bows on NBC. SEPTEMBER 28: "60 Minutes" debuts on CBS...tick...tick...tick.

1 9 6 9

FEBRUARY 9: CBS presents the Royal Shakespeare Company's production of "A Midsummers Night's Dream" starring Diana Rigg, David Warner and Helen Mirren. June 15: "Hee Haw " premieres on CBS. JULY 20: Approximately 700 million people around the world watch Apollo 11 land on the moon, and Neil Armstrong taking his historic first step. SEPTEMBER 14: "The Bill Cosby Show" commences its CBS run. SEPTEMBER 26: "The Brady Bunch" first airs on ABC. OCTOBER 5: PBS airs the first of 26 chapters of "The Forsyte Saga." NOVEMBER 10: "Sesame Street" commences its landmark journey on PBS stations. DECEMBER 17: Tiny Tim marries Miss Vicki on Johnny Carson's "Tonight Show."

Decca, 1969 UK

SEPTEMBER 10: Mary Tyler Moore premieres her own show on CBS. OCTOBER 5: Alistair Cooke is hired by WGBH Boston to introduce new imported British TV dramas under the umbrella of "Masterpiece Theatre."

1 9 7 1

JANUARY 12: "All in the Family" premieres on CBS. MARCH 17: After 23 years, "The Ed Sullivan Show" comes to an end. JUNE 7: After stating how healthy he is, J.I. Rodale, publisher of the health magazine "Prevention" dies of a heart attack while being interviewed on the "Dick Cavett Show." A TV first. SEPTEMBER 15: NBC debuts "Columbo" starring Peter Falk.

1 9 7 2

MAY15: As news cameras roll, George Wallace is shot in plain view while campaigning for the Democratic presidential nomination. SEPTEMBER 17: "M*A*S*H*" premieres on CBS. OCTOBER 27: "Captain Kangaroo" hops on the screen for the 5,000th time. NOVEMBER 8: Home Box Office commences broadcasting with a test group of 365 subscribers in Wilkes-Barre, PA. In five years, the subscriber base tops 1,000,000, heralding the start of the Cable Age.

1 9 7 3

OCTOBER 24: Kojak solves his first crime on CBS. DECEMBER 19: Johnny Carson creates a national panic buying binge of toilet paper after announcing that it is in short supply.

JVC, 1975 Japan

1 9 7 4

An era ends. The last original episode of "Here's Lucy" appears on CBS.

1 9 7 5

The World Heavyweight Title fight between Joe Frazier and Muhammad Ali is beamed via satellite to the US for cable showing on HBO. Hundreds of thousands of subscribers confirm the viability of cable pay-per-view.

1 9 7 6

DECEMBER 17: WTCG-TV Atlanta begins satellite transmissions of its regular scheduling to four cable systems, thus becoming the first Superstation. Three years later WTCG (Turner Communications Group) changes its call letters to WTBS.

JACK BENNY ON "THE TONIGHT SHOW STARRING JOHNNY CARSON"

Enjoy true-to-life Color from RCA Victor with Solid Copper Circuit dependability

Most true-to-life color . . . so natural and sharp you'll compare it to color motion pictures. And the High Fidelity tube gives you the brightest pictures ever from RCA Victor.

Dependable RCA Solid Copper Circuits replace old-fashioned "hand wiring"—eliminate over 200 possible trouble spots. This means fewer service headaches, greater reliability.

Specially designed circuitry of this kind is used in space satellites. More TV servicemen own RCA Victor Color TV than all other leading makes combined.

RCA pioneered and perfected Color TV . . . is the world's most experienced maker of color sets. More people own RCA Victor Color TV than all other brands combined. See why—at your dealer's now!

RCA SOLID COPPER CIRCUITS REPLACE OLD-FASHIONED "HAND WIRING" FOR GREATER DEPENDABILITY, BETTER TV PERFORMANCE.

JVC, 1975 Japan

1977

ANUARY 23: "Roots" becomes the most watched TV show in history with 12 hours over eight consecutive nights. The final two hours is ewed by an estimated 80,000,000 people. APRIL: There are now 71,000,000 homes in the US with at least one TV. Nearly half have two ets and of those nearly 75% own a color set. 710 commercial TV stations and 252 public stations now broadcast in America.

1978

PRIL 2: "Dallas" bows on CBS. OCTOBER 1: Television's most ambitious project to date, the 25-hour, $25 million production of James ichener's "Centennial" premieres its first episode on NBC. Richard Chamberlain is the star.

1979

OVEMBER 29: ABC's Ted Koppel fills in for the usual anchorman for "The Iran Crisis" and "Nightline" is born. DECEMBER 20: "Knots anding" first airs on CBS.

Panasonic, 1969 Japan

1980

MARCH 16: The TeleCaption decoder, permitting deaf viewers to read closed-captioning, is introduced. Sixteen hours of network programming using the service begin on ABC, NBC and PBS.

1 9 8 2

SEPTEMBER 30: "Cheers" opens its doors on NBC.

1 9 8 3

FEBRUARY 28: The last original "M*A*S*H*" episode is watched on CBS by 107,000,000 viewers in the US. The 2½ hour special is the biggest audience grabber ever. The show's 251 episodes garnered 14 Emmys (from 99 nominations) over its 11-year life.

1 9 8 5

Metromedia TV stations are sold to Rupert Murdoch who creates the new Fox TV Network, the first viable, commercial US network to be created in 37 years.

1 9 8 7

"Married With Children" premieres on the Fox network and the modern family from hell is an instant success.

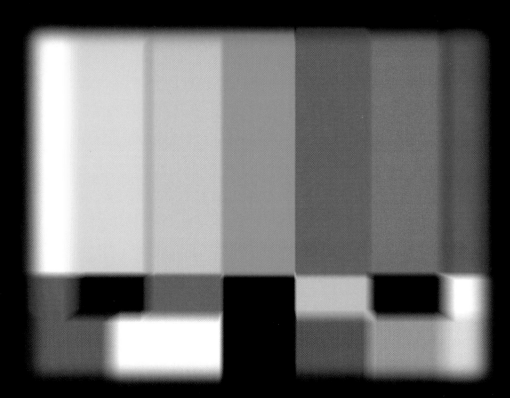

1988

OCTOBER 18: "Roseanne" debuts on ABC.

1989

JULY 23: Fox TV, the fourth channel, beats out ABC, NBC and CBS for the time slots of "America's Most Wanted" and "Totally Hidden Video." A ratings first for the network. AUGUST 26: *TV Guide*'s sexy cover, featuring the slimline Oprah Winfrey, is exposed as a fraudulent composite, featuring Ann-Margret's body.

1990

September 23: After five years in the making, the epic "Civil War" series premieres on PBS. A landmark achievement in 11 one-hour episodes.

1992

MAY 22: Johnny Carson leaves his hosting role on "The Tonight Show" after 30 years, a brilliant TV achievement.

1995

JANUARY 31: Court TV, the cable station, carries the trial of O.J. Simpson, accused of two brutal slayings, from gavel to gavel until the verdict on October 3rd. Other channels televise selected incidents throughout. Historic television coverage on an unprecedented level. The judge in the subsequent 1996 civil case banned TV coverage.

GPX, 1990 Japan

Baird, Televisor, 1920 UK
page 15

General Electric, Octagon 1928 USA
page 15

Western Television Scanner, 1929 USA
page 16

Baird, 1936 UK
page 19

Cosser, 1936 UK
page 21

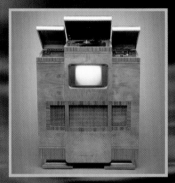

HMV, 1937 UK
page 23

HMV, 1938 UK
page 24

RCA TKR-12, 1939 USA
page 11

Dynatron, 1939 UK
page 26

General Electric, 1939 USA
page 28

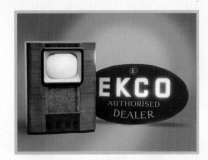

Ekco, 1939 UK
page 31

RCA, 1939/1946 USA
page 35

DuMont Clifton, 1945 USA
page 33

RCA, 1946 USA
page 39

RCA, 1947 USA/
Sony, 1959 Japan
page 12

Farnsworth, 1947 USA
page 41

Philco, 1947 USA
page 44

Viewtone, 1947 USA
page 45

Admiral, 1947 USA
page 37

Admiral, 1947/1948 USA
page 36

Motorola, 1947/1949 USA
page 40

DuMont, 1948 USA
page 47

General Electric,
1948 USA
page 48

Philco, 1948 USA
page 49

Philco, 1948 USA
page 51

Hallicrafters, 1948 USA
page 52

RCA, 1948 USA
page 53

Scott, 1948 USA
page 54

Stromberg Carlson,
1948 USA
page 55

Raytheon, 1948 USA
page 67

General Electric
1948/1949 USA
page 44

Baird, 1948 UK
Caperhart, 1949 USA
page 46

Motorola, 1948 USA
G.E.C., 1950 USA
page 51

Philco, 1949 USA
page 57

Hofman, 1949 USA
page 59

DuMont, 1949 USA
page 60

Fada, 1949 USA
page 62

Radiola, 1949 USA
page 63

La Voix de Son Maitre,
1949 France
page 66

Motorola, 1949 USA
page 68

Emerson, 1949 USA
page 69

Truetone, 1950 USA
Firestone, 1950 USA
Airline, 1949 USA
Sentinels, 1948 USA
page 61

Crosley, 1950 USA
page 70

Baird, 1950 UK
page 71

Stromberg Carlson
1950 USA
page 73

Raytheon, 1950 USA
page 73

RCA, 1950 USA
page 73

Emerson, 1950 USA
page 74/75

Motorola, 1950 USA
page 77

General Electric,
1950 USA
page 78

Pye, 1950 UK
page 79

Bush, 1950/1954 UK
page 64

Zenith, 1951 USA
page 82

RCA, 1954 USA
page 85

123

Watt, 1956 Italy
page 87

Wega, 1956 Germany
page 88/89

Zenith, 1956 USA
page 91

RCA, 1957 USA
page 95

Teleavia, 1957 Italy
page 97

RCA, 1957 USA
page 98

RCA, c.1958 USA
page 93

Philco, Safari,
1959 USA
page 99

Philco Tandem, 1959 USA
page 100

Philco Pedestal, 1959 USA
page 101

RCA, 1959 USA
page 103

Philco, 1962 USA
page 107

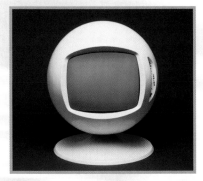

Decca, 1969 UK
page 108

Panasonic, 1969 Japan
page 113

JVC Videosphere, 1975 Japan
page 110

JVC Videocube, 1975 Japan
page 112

Fergusson, 1986
(Repro) UK
page 11

GPX, 1990 Japan
page 116

ACKNOWLEDGMENTS

For their generous assistance in the production of this book,
grateful thanks are due to Garry Brod, Frank Cardoza Jr, Dennis Clark,
Susan Shearer, Jery Simpson and Kay Tornborg.
Particular thanks are due to Kosh, Sandy Lieberson
and Bernard Sampson who graciously supplied the TVs.

Page 80, "Televiewing is a Science": first published in Esquire magazine, March, 1950.
reprinted courtesy of Esquire magazine and the Hearst Corporation.
Page 84, cartoon: first published in Esquire magazine, February, 1950.
Reprinted courtesy of Esquire magazine and the Hearst Corporation.
Page 92, Saturday Evening Post illustration:
reprinted courtesy The Curtis Publishing Company

PHILIP COLLINS

PHILIP COLLINS *writes books on popular culture and screenplays*

for fun and profit in Los Angeles, California.

Other Fillip Books *by Philip Collins:*

Radios: The Golden Age

Smokerama

Radios Redux

The Art of the Cocktail

Pastime

Classic Cocktails of the Prohibition Era

Cigar Bizarre

Radios: Funiture That Talks

OOPS!
CABLE TROUBLE
KING-TV

photograph by Kay Tornborg

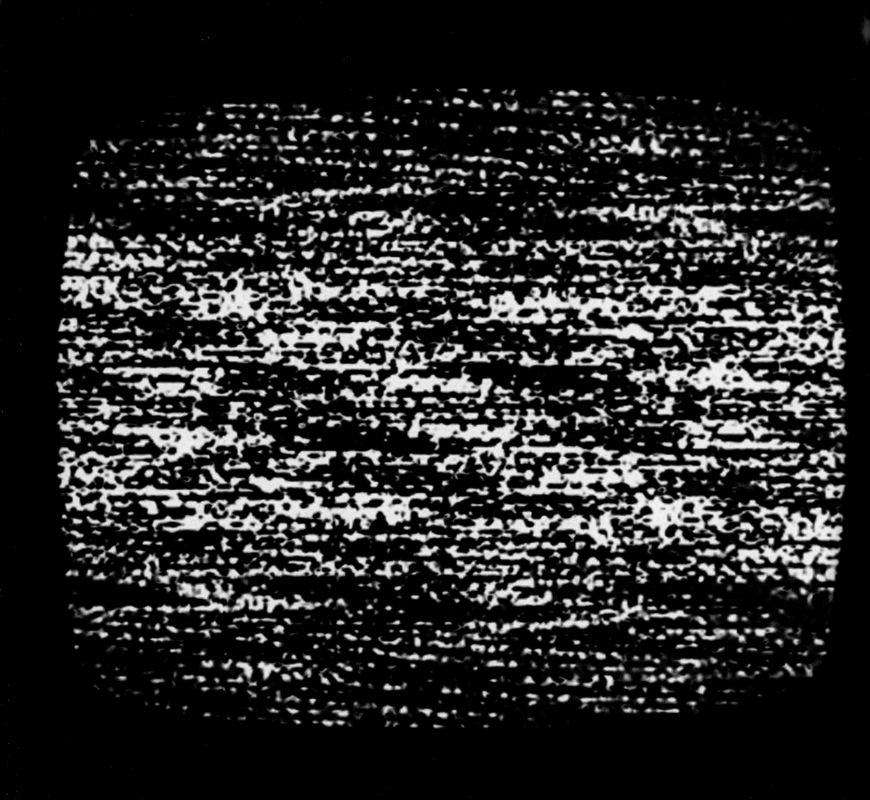

"I didn't think it would end like this."

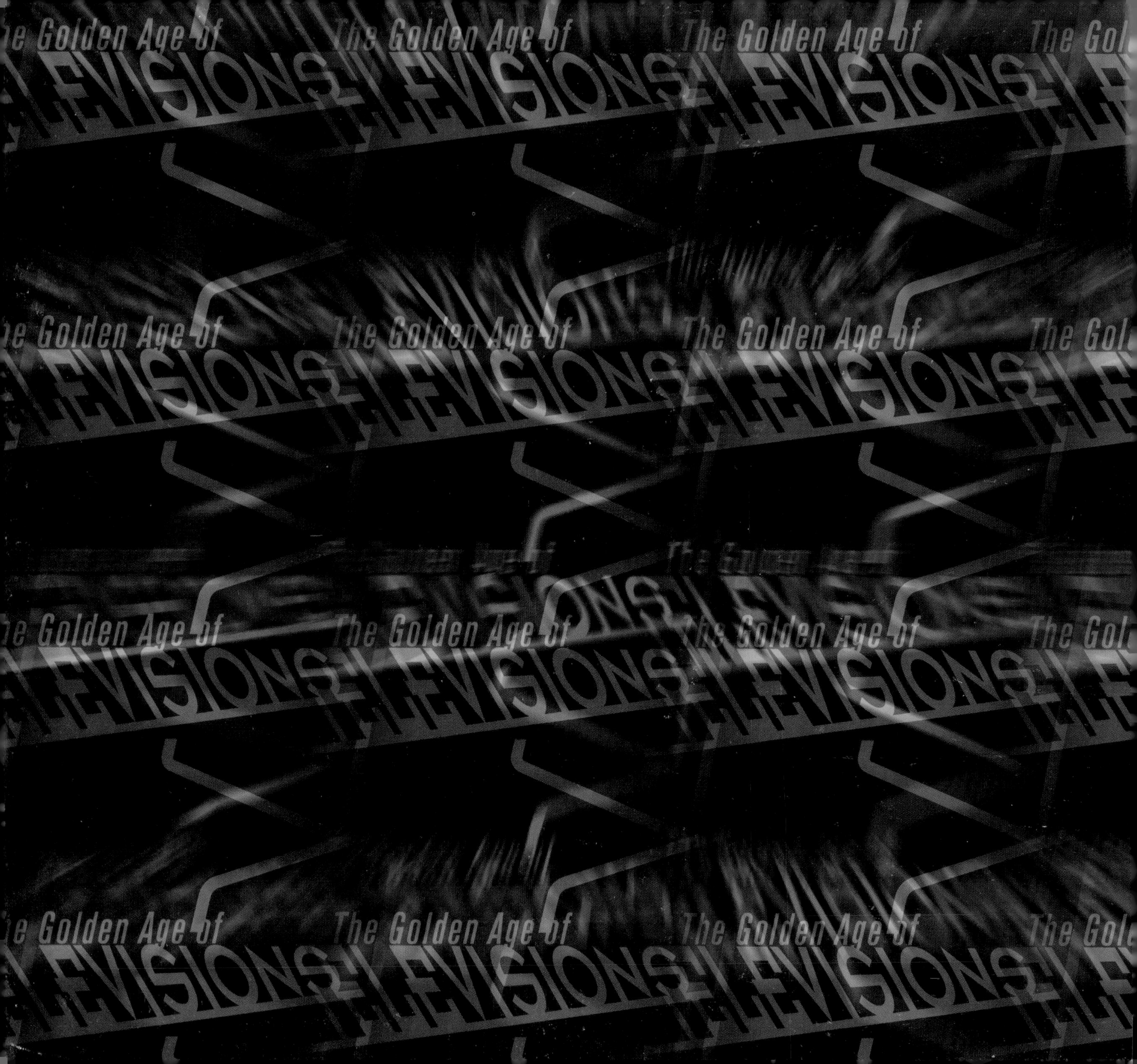
The Golden Age of
TELEVISIONS